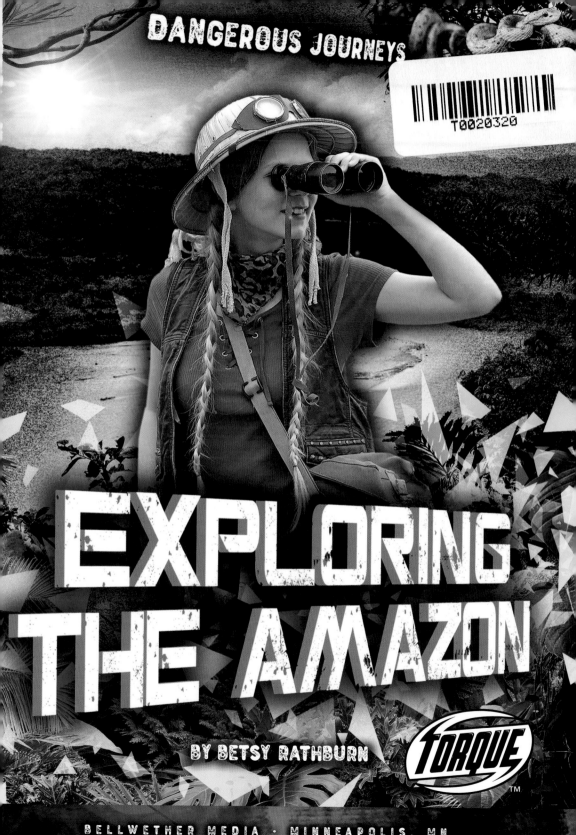

DANGEROUS JOURNEYS

T0020320

EXPLORING THE AMAZON

BY BETSY RATHBURN

TORQUE
TM

BELLWETHER MEDIA · MINNEAPOLIS, MN

™

Torque brims with excitement
perfect for thrill-seekers of all kinds.
Discover daring survival skills, explore
uncharted worlds, and marvel at mighty
engines and extreme sports. In *Torque* books,
anything can happen. Are you ready?

This edition first published in 2023 by Bellwether Media, Inc.

No part of this publication may be reproduced in whole or in part without
written permission of the publisher. For information regarding permission,
write to Bellwether Media, Inc., Attention: Permissions Department,
6012 Blue Circle Drive, Minnetonka, MN 55343.

Library of Congress Cataloging-in-Publication Data

LC record for Exploring the Amazon available at:
https://lccn.loc.gov/2022012969

Editor: Kieran Downs   Designer: Josh Brink

Printed in the United States of America, North Mankato, MN.

TABLE OF CONTENTS

A JUNGLE JOURNEY

A long boat lands on the riverbank. A group of explorers steps out. They study the thick forest before them. How will they make it through?

One explorer spots a gap in the trees. It leads to a narrow dirt path. Thick roots and vines cover it. But the explorers hike on. They will explore the Amazon!

FINDING THE FOREST

AMAZON RAIN FOREST

The Amazon is a huge **rain forest** found in eight countries in South America. It is the largest rain forest in the world!

The Amazon is one of the most **biodiverse** places on Earth. Millions of plant and animal **species** live there. Many live along the Amazon River and its **tributaries**.

AMAZON RAIN FOREST MAP

AMAZON RAIN FOREST = ◆

Millions of people live in the Amazon. Large cities dot the region. There are also many areas controlled by **indigenous** groups.

MANAUS, BRAZIL

FLOODING

But much of the Amazon is still unexplored. The thick rain forest makes it hard to travel in some areas. Heavy rains can wash away roads and flood rivers. Amazon plants and animals can also be dangerous.

People have explored the Amazon for hundreds of years. In the past, many explorers looked for gold. Others wanted to spread religion.

Today, some scientists explore the Amazon to study wildlife and **climate change**. They record information and take **samples**. Others look for signs of past peoples. They dig for ancient tools, art, and other items.

SCIENTIST

IN 2017, SCIENTISTS UNCOVERED HUGE CLIFF PAINTINGS IN THE AMAZON. THEY SHOW PEOPLE AND ANIMALS. THE PAINTINGS ARE OVER 12,000 YEARS OLD!

NOTABLE EXPLORER

NAME: SYDNEY POSSUELO

BORN: APRIL 19, 1940

JOURNEY: CONTACTED INDIGENOUS GROUPS IN THE AMAZON RAIN FOREST AND WORKED WITH GOVERNMENTS TO PROTECT THE GROUPS FROM OUTSIDERS

RESULTS: GOVERNMENTS HAVE SET ASIDE LAND FOR INDIGENOUS GROUPS, STOPPED LOGGING THEIR LAND, AND STOPPED UNWANTED VISITORS FROM CONTACTING THEM

PLANNING AND PREPARATION

Amazon explorers must prepare before they set out on their journey. Many get **vaccinations** to prevent diseases. They may train to make sure their bodies can handle the heat of the rain forest.

Explorers must plan their path, too. They study maps. They avoid dangerous areas. They may hire boats or guides.

TASTY CLAY

PARROTS LICK CLAY FROM AMAZON RIVERBANKS TO STAY HEALTHY. SCIENTISTS TAKE BOATS TO STUDY THE CLAY LICKS!

PLANNING YOUR JOURNEY

GET VACCINATIONS

PLAN ROUTES

HIRE BOATS OR TOUR GUIDES

GATHER SUPPLIES

Explorers should also learn about Amazon wildlife. Dangerous animals make their homes in the forest and waters. Explorers should know how to avoid them.

Explorers should gather gear, too. Waterproof clothes keep them dry. Sunscreen protects against the hot sun. Bug spray and mosquito nets keep **insects** away. Head lamps help explorers see at night.

INTO THE AMAZON

Many explorers begin their trips in cities. Others enter the Amazon by boat. Explorers use maps and compasses to **navigate**. Without them, it is easy to get lost!

Explorers must watch out for dangerous wildlife as they travel. **Poisonous** frogs crawl on the forest floor. Piranhas and eels swim through rivers. Caimans wait on riverbanks.

POISON DART FROG

SECRETS IN THE SOIL

TERRA PRETA IS BLACK SOIL THAT IS GOOD FOR FARMING. IT IS FOUND IN MANY PARTS OF THE AMAZON. SCIENTISTS BELIEVE IT IS A SIGN THAT THE FOREST WAS ONCE FILLED WITH FARMLAND!

CAIMANS

Rainy weather can cause problems for explorers. Floods can wash away campsites and supplies. Camping on high ground helps keep explorers and their gear dry.

Rain also brings out more mosquitoes. These insects can carry **parasites** that cause **malaria**. Explorers must avoid their bites! Some take pills that make it harder to catch malaria.

MORE MALARIA

EVERY YEAR, OVER 1 MILLION AMAZON TREES ARE CUT DOWN TO CLEAR LAND FOR HOUSING. MORE PEOPLE MOVE TO THE AMAZON. MORE MOSQUITOES CAN LIVE IN OPEN SPACES. MALARIA SPREADS MORE QUICKLY!

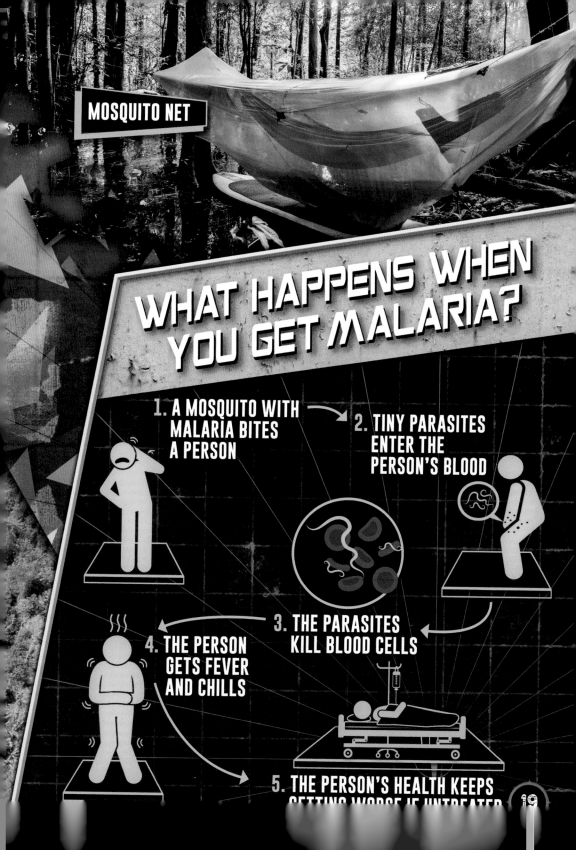

MOSQUITO NET

WHAT HAPPENS WHEN YOU GET MALARIA?

1. A MOSQUITO WITH MALARIA BITES A PERSON

2. TINY PARASITES ENTER THE PERSON'S BLOOD

3. THE PARASITES KILL BLOOD CELLS

4. THE PERSON GETS FEVER AND CHILLS

5. THE PERSON'S HEALTH KEEPS GETTING WORSE IF UNTREATED

Prepared explorers easily survive the Amazon. They chop through rain forest plants and paddle through muddy rivers. They climb high into the **canopy** or dig deep for signs of ancient life.

The Amazon is an exciting place to explore. Scientists who go there bring back important information. They uncover facts about the earth, its history, and its wildlife!

GLOSSARY

biodiverse—having a lot of different plants and animals

canopy—the uppermost level of the rain forest

climate change—a human-caused change in Earth's weather due to warming temperatures

indigenous—related to the earliest known people who lived in an area

insects—small animals with six legs and hard outer bodies; an insect's body is divided into three parts.

malaria—a disease of the blood that causes sickness and death; malaria can be carried by mosquitoes.

navigate—to find a way from place to place

parasites—living things that survive on or in other living things; parasites offer nothing for the food and protection they receive.

poisonous—causing sickness or death when touched or eaten by animals

rain forest—a thick, green forest that receives a lot of rain

samples—small amounts of things that give information about where they were taken from

species—types of plants and animals

tributaries—streams that flow into larger streams, rivers, or lakes

vaccinations—substances that are put into people or animals to protect them against certain diseases

TO LEARN MORE

AT THE LIBRARY

Dufresne, Emilie. *Endangered Animals in the Rain Forest*. New York, N.Y.: PowerKids Press, 2022.

Kenney, Karen Latchana. *Rain Forests*. Minneapolis, Minn.: Bellwether Media, 2022.

Vonder Brink, Tracy. *Protecting the Amazon Rainforest*. Lake Elmo, Minn.: Focus Readers, 2020.

ON THE WEB

FACTSURFER

Factsurfer.com gives you a safe, fun way to find more information.

1. Go to www.factsurfer.com

2. Enter "exploring the Amazon" into the search box and click 🔍.

3. Select your book cover to see a list of related content.

INDEX

The images in this book are reproduced through the courtesy of: Photo-Art-Lortie, front cover (hero); Ondrej Prosicky, front cover (snake); Allen.G, front cover (background), pp. 3, 23; Aurelvia, front cover (palm leaves); Chansom Pantip, front cover (foliage, fiddle leaf); Nature Design, front cover (vines); Alida Latham/ DanitaDelimont/ Alamy, p. 4; R. Tyler Gross/ Aurora Open RF/ Alamy, p. 5; Gustavo Frazao, p. 6; Dr Morley Read, pp. 8, 9; Melba Photo Agency/ Alamy, p. 10; The Washington Post/ Getty Images, p. 11; Scott Wallace, p. 11 (Sydney Possuelo); SL-Photography, p. 11 (treeline); Click and Photo, p. 12; Martin Lindsay/ Alamy, p. 13 (parrots); Halfpoint, p. 13 (vaccination); Alexander Lukatskiy, p. 13 (plan routes); A.P.S.Photography, p. 13 (hire boats); Lucky Business, p. 13 (gather supplies); Sergey Uryadnikov, p. 14; Ammit/ Alamy, p. 15; Ricardo Lima/ Getty Images, p. 16; Dirk Ercken, p. 17 (frog); Ondrej Prosicky, p. 17 (caiman); Nigel Dickinson/ Alamy, p. 18; Nowaczyk, p. 19; Leremy, p. 19 (icons); Puwadol Jaturawutthichai, p. 19 (blood cell); WhiteDragon, p. 19 (parasite); Pete Oxford/ Alamy, p. 20; Konrad Wothe/ Alamy, p. 21.